Let's Get Mapping!

Mapping the Land and Weather

Melanie Waldron

Raintree

Chicago, Illinois

Edited by Nancy Dickmann and Abby Colich
Designed by Victoria Allen
Original illustrations © 2013
Illustrated by HL Studios
Picture research by Ruth Blair
Originated by Capstone Global Library Limited
Printed and bound in China by CTPS

17 16 15 14 13 12
10 9 8 7 6 5 4 3 2 1

**Library of Congress Cataloging-in-Publication
Data**
Waldron, Melanie.
  Mapping the land and weather / Melanie
Waldron.
      p. cm.—(Let's get mapping!)
  Includes bibliographical references and index.
  ISBN 978-1-4109-4902-8 (hb)—ISBN 978-1-4109-
4909-7 (pb) 1. Cartography—Juvenile literature.
2. Weather—Maps—Juvenile literature. I. Title.
  GA105.6.W35 2013
  526—dc23   2012008513

Acknowledgments
We would like to thank the following for
permission to reproduce photographs:
Alamy: pp. 4 (© citypix), 13 (© Danita Delimont),
18 (© Robert Adrian Hillman), 19 (© DCPhoto);
Corbis: p. 15 (© Ocean); Science Photo Library:
pp. 24 (GARY HINCKS), 26 (PLANETOBSERVER);
Shutterstock: pp. 6 (© PavelSvoboda),
10 (© J. McCormick), 17 (© Pigprox),
23 (© wdeon), 25 (© Richard Thornton);
Superstock: pp. 5 (© Stock Connection);
USGS: p. 27.

Cover photograph of a topological map looking
north from Lake Mead, Arizona, reproduced with
permission from iStockphoto (© Jami Garrison).

Background and design features reproduced
with permission from Shutterstock.

Every effort has been made to contact
copyright holders of any material reproduced
in this book. Any omissions will be rectified
in subsequent printings if notice is given to
the publisher.

All the Internet addresses (URLs) given in this
book were valid at the time of going to press.
However, due to the dynamic nature of the
Internet, some addresses may have changed,
or sites may have changed or ceased to exist
since publication. While the author and
publisher regret any inconvenience this may
cause readers, no responsibility for any such
changes can be accepted by either the author
or the publisher.

Contents

Some words appear in the text in bold, **like this**. You can find out what they mean by looking in the glossary.

A World of Maps

A map is a flat drawing of an area of land. Maps can show lots of different things, including buildings and roads. They can show **natural features** such as rivers, forests, and rocks. They can also show you other types of information, such as the average temperatures across a country.

Map makers have been mapping locations for centuries. This map of modern-day Mexico was drawn in 1606.

Political, physical, and thematic maps

There are lots of different types of maps. Some maps are called **political maps**. These usually show the **borders** between countries. They also show the capital cities and other large towns and cities.

Physical maps show what the land is like, including its height and shape. Physical maps can also show things like the buildings and roads that are on the land. **Thematic maps** show information about places on the land. For example, a map showing the average price of a house in each region of a country would be a thematic map.

CARTOGRAPHY

Making maps is called cartography. People who make maps are called **cartographers**.

The Shape of the Land

Many physical maps try to show what the land actually looks like. This includes the hills, valleys, mountains, flat land, and everything in between. Cartographers need to find ways to show these **3D** shapes on flat paper or on a computer screen.

Cartographers use clever ways to show land that is not flat on maps.

Symbols and shade

Some maps use **symbols** to show hilly areas and mountains. Symbols are little pictures or shapes that represent something. For example, a small triangle might be used to represent a mountain.

Another way to show the shape of the land is to use shade. Shading some parts of the map make it look as if some areas are put in shade by high land or mountains.

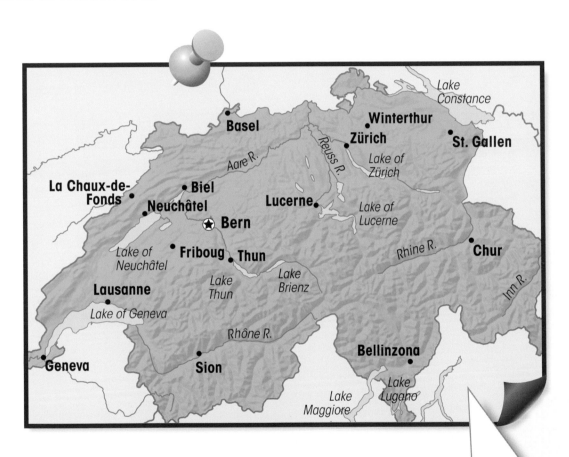

MAPPING MOUNT EVEREST

It took around 50 years to map India—including Mount Everest, the highest mountain on Earth. George Everest led the mapping survey. The mountain is named after him.

Relief maps, such as this one of Switzerland, use shadows to show high land. Can you find any flat areas here, where there are no shadows?

Colors and Contours

Color-shaded relief maps use different colors to show how high each piece of land is. Low-lying land is shown as one color. As the land height rises, different bands of color are used to show this. Very mountainous areas often have white at the very top, which looks a bit like snow.

This map of India shows where the land is highest. Use the **key** to figure out what height of land the colors are showing.

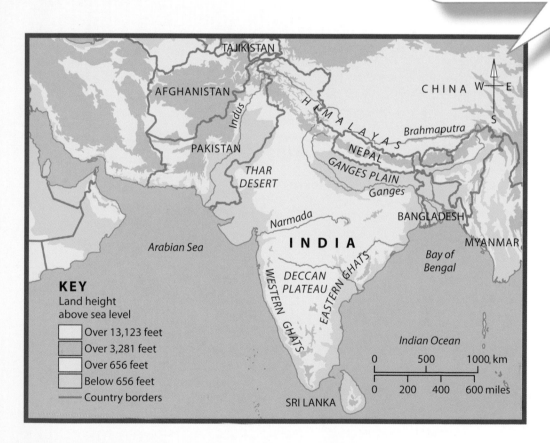

KEY

Land height above sea level

- Over 13,123 feet
- Over 3,281 feet
- Over 656 feet
- Below 656 feet
- Country borders

Contour lines on maps show the height of the land in detail. Contour lines follow the land at the same height above sea level. For example, a 750-foot (230-meter) contour line would follow the land that is 750 feet above sea level. See the contour lines in the map on page 9.

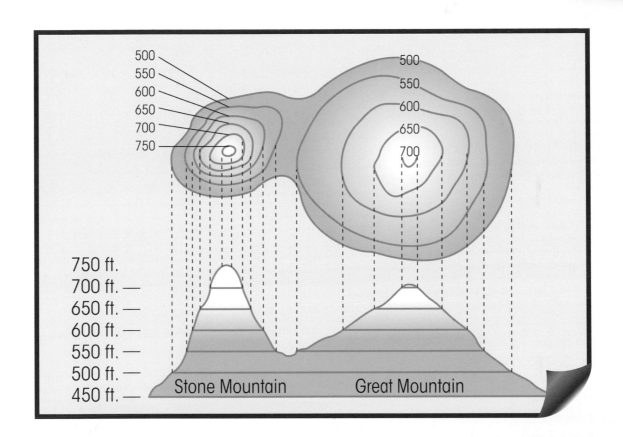

500
550
600
650
700
750

500
550
600
650
700

750 ft.
700 ft. —
650 ft. —
600 ft. —
550 ft. —
500 ft. —
450 ft. —

Stone Mountain   Great Mountain

STEEP LAND, FLAT LAND

Contour lines are spaced at intervals. For
example, one line might show land that is
30 feet (9 meters) higher than the next line. Steep
land is shown by contour lines packed closely
together, because there is only a short distance
before the land height rises 30 feet. Land that is
quite flat is shown by widely spaced contour lines,
because there is a further distance to go before
the land height rises 30 feet.

Bodies of Water

World maps show oceans, large lakes, and large rivers such as the Amazon, the Mississippi, and the Ganges. Rivers are usually shown on maps as a blue line. When you are using a map of your local area, it is useful if the map shows all the bodies of water in detail. These include smaller rivers, lakes, and marshes.

Maps can also show any structures that have been built on or around bodies of water, such as bridges. It is very useful to know where bridges are so that you can plan where to cross a river. Many maps use small symbols to represent different structures.

In the area shown below, there are many different bodies of water, including rivers and marshes. Maps can show us where these things are located.

This simple sketch map shows physical features seen in the photo on page 10. You can use the key to understand what the symbols on the map mean.

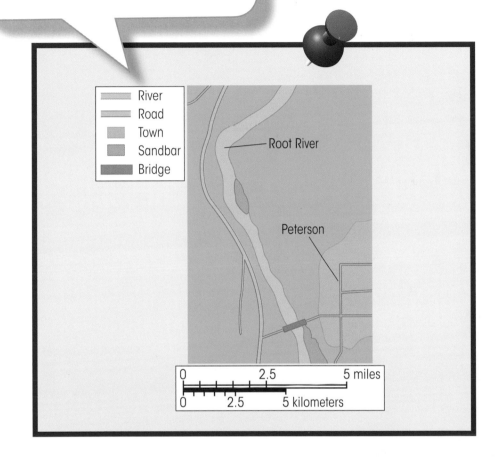

River
Road
Town
Sandbar
Bridge

Root River

Peterson

0   2.5   5 miles
0   2.5   5 kilometers

WINDING DOWN THE RIVER

Sometimes people use rivers as paths to follow on a map. In the United States, a popular driving trip involves following the Mississippi River from its northern beginnings in Minnesota all the way south to the Gulf of Mexico.

Mapping Seas and Coasts

Some maps do not show any detail about the land at all! Instead, they show lots of information about the sea. World maps can show how **ocean currents** move. Ocean currents are huge bodies of water that usually flow in the same direction all the time. They can contain warm or cold water, and they can have a big effect on weather and sea life.

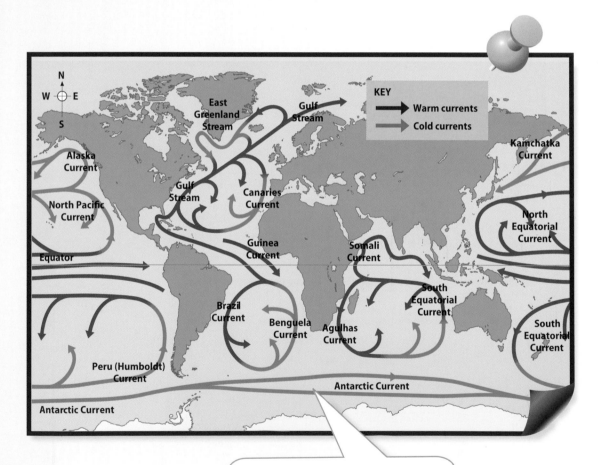

This map shows how warm and cold ocean currents move around the world.

Underwater detail

Some maps contain a lot of detail about the shape of the coastline and the depth of the sea around the coast. Sailors use these maps to safely steer their ships and boats around the coast. They need to know that the water is deep enough.

SONAR SURVEYING

Some ships are made specifically to survey and map the seabed. They often use **sonar** (sound waves) to do this. A computer sends out a sound signal. This signal is reflected back once it hits a surface. The computer can then figure out the depth of the water along the seabed.

Maps of the coast help sailors avoid rocks that could cause damage.

Mapping the Climate

The **climate** of an area is the usual type of weather conditions you would expect to find there. Climate includes temperature, rainfall, wind speed, and hours of sunshine. There are different **climate zones** around the world.

World maps can show the different climate zones. Maps of **continents** and large countries can also show how the climate might be different in some areas. Maps of smaller areas, such as a village, would not be useful for showing climate. This is because the climate would be mostly the same for the whole area.

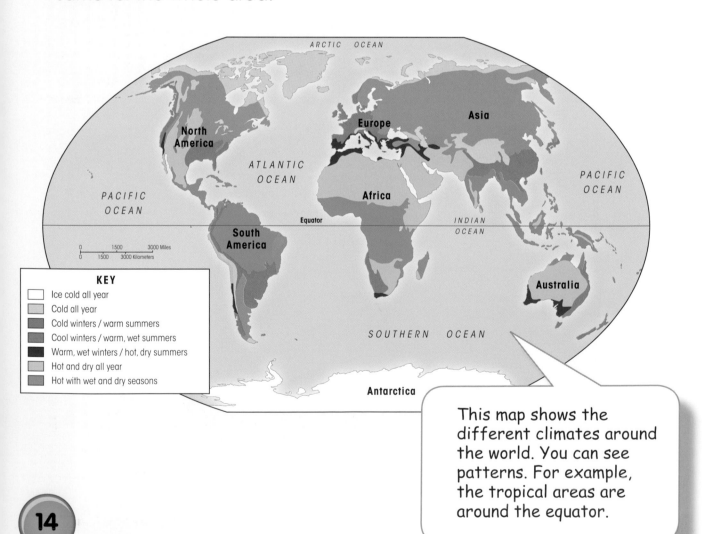

KEY

- Ice cold all year
- Cold all year
- Cold winters / warm summers
- Cool winters / warm, wet summers
- Warm, wet winters / hot, dry summers
- Hot and dry all year
- Hot with wet and dry seasons

This map shows the different climates around the world. You can see patterns. For example, the tropical areas are around the equator.

Latitude and climate

Climates around the world are linked to **latitude**, which is the distance north or south of the **equator**. Lines of latitude are imaginary lines that circle around Earth. The equator is a line of latitude. It circles all the way around the middle of Earth.

LINES OF LONGITUDE

Lines of **longitude** run from the top to the bottom of Earth. Each one passes through the North and South Poles.

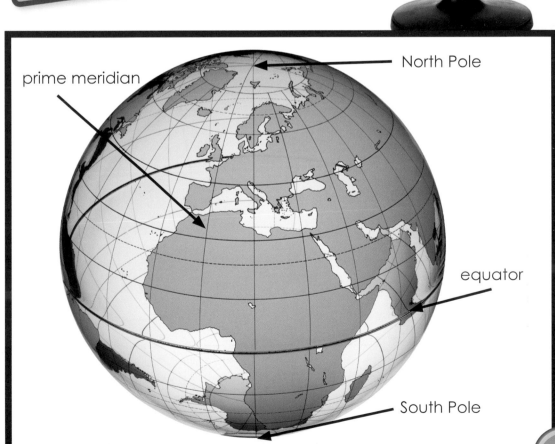

prime meridian

North Pole

equator

South Pole

Mapping the Weather

The weather in an area can change day-by-day, sometimes hour-by-hour. Weather maps are much more detailed than climate maps. They also change much more often—even several times a day—as the weather changes.

It is really useful to be able to read weather maps. They usually use symbols to show what the weather is like. You can look at the symbols for your area to help you decide what the weather is like. You can then decide the best clothes to wear!

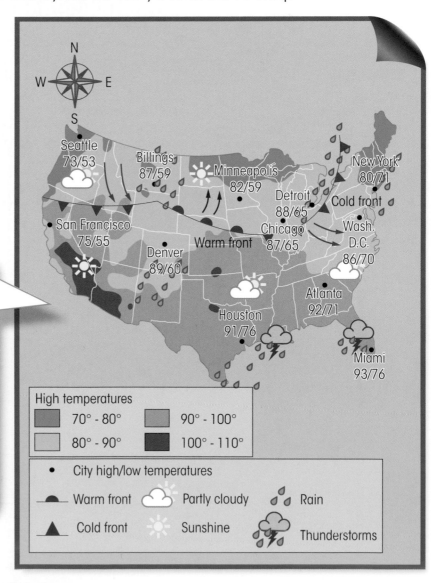

This is the kind of weather map you might see for the United States. You can use the symbols to figure out what the weather will be in your area on a certain day.

High temperatures

70° - 80°	90° - 100°
80° - 90°	100° - 110°

- City high/low temperatures

Warm front   Partly cloudy   Rain

Cold front   Sunshine   Thunderstorms

Windy weather

Weather maps often show the direction of wind using an arrow. The arrow points in the direction that the wind is blowing. The wind speed is sometimes written as a number attached to the arrow. In the United States, this number is measured in miles per hour.

Weather maps can tell you if the wind in your area is strong enough for kite flying.

Weather Forecasts

Weather forecast maps try to show us what the weather might be like later in the day, the next day, or later in the week. Scientists try to predict the weather. They use patterns of air pressure to help them do this. Air pressure is the force of the air pressing down on Earth. Different air pressure can cause different weather conditions. Wind is created when air moves from areas of high pressure to areas of low pressure.

Isobars are lines that link all the areas with the same air pressure. They work in a similar way to contour lines. When isobars are close together, that means the air pressure is changing a lot over a small area. This means that the weather will be very windy.

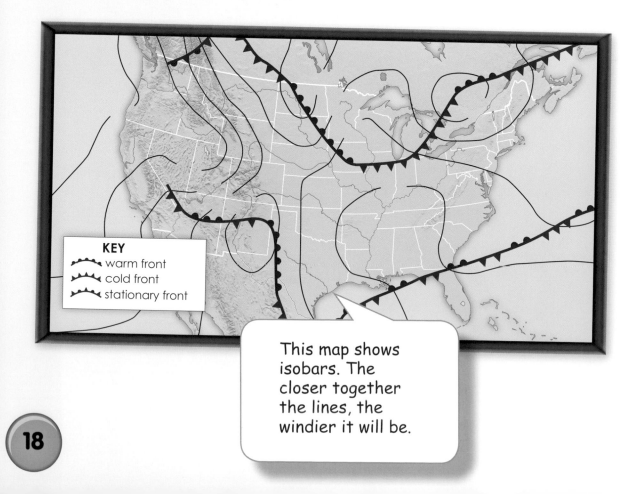

KEY
- warm front
- cold front
- stationary front

This map shows isobars. The closer together the lines, the windier it will be.

CELL PHONE FORECASTS

It is important for people out walking or cycling in mountainous areas to know the weather forecast. To help them stay safe, they can download up-to-date and very detailed weather forecasts onto their cell phones.

Mapping Nature

Across the world, the different climates mean that different types of plants and animals can live there. An area of Earth where certain groups of plants and animals live is called a **biome**. Some plants and animals can cope with living in very cold, very hot, or very dry biomes. Others need less harsh conditions to live in.

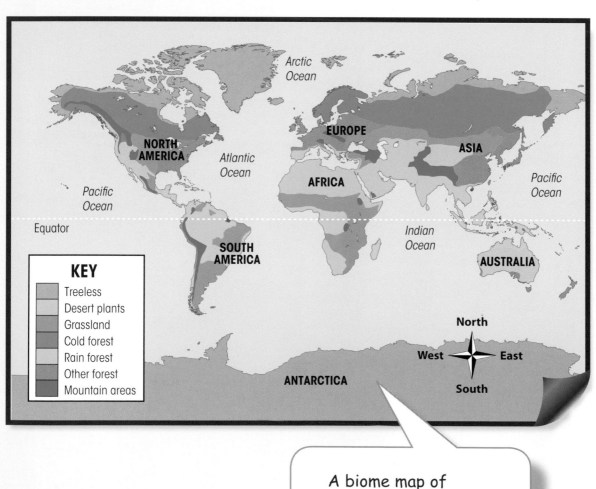

Arctic Ocean

NORTH AMERICA

EUROPE

ASIA

Atlantic Ocean

AFRICA

Pacific Ocean

Pacific Ocean

Equator

SOUTH AMERICA

Indian Ocean

AUSTRALIA

KEY
- Treeless
- Desert plants
- Grassland
- Cold forest
- Rain forest
- Other forest
- Mountain areas

ANTARCTICA

North
West — East
South

A biome map of the world can tell us where we would expect to find certain plants and animals.

BIOMES AND CLIMATES

Look at the map of world climates on page 14 and compare this with the biome map. You will see some similarities, because biomes are affected by climate. In the Arctic, the climate is cold. The soil is frozen for much of the year, so only very small and tough plants can grow there.

Mapping animals

We can use maps to look in detail at the places certain wild animals live. This is useful when trying to protect **endangered** animals. If we can see that the areas they live in are smaller now than in the past, we can work to protect those areas.

The green areas on this map show where wolves live today. In the past, they also used to live in the pink areas.

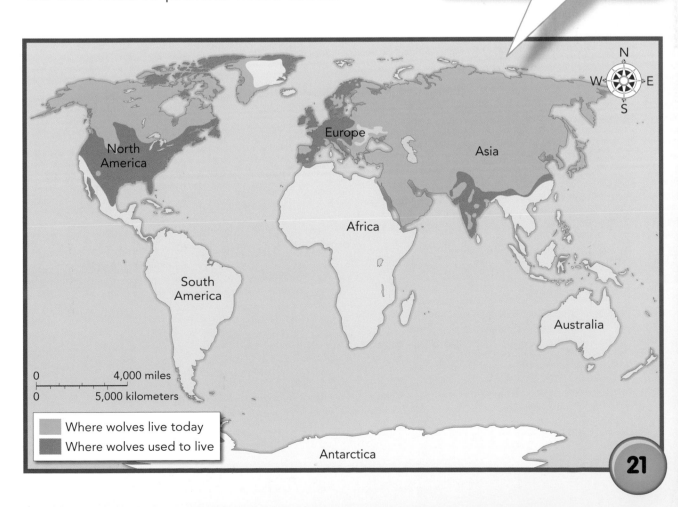

North America

Europe

Asia

Africa

South America

Australia

0   4,000 miles

0   5,000 kilometers

Where wolves live today
Where wolves used to live

Antarctica

Mapping Tectonics

Tectonics is all about the movement of the surface of Earth. This surface is made up of lots of enormous pieces called plates. Where these plates meet, there are often volcanoes and earthquakes. It is important to know where these areas are so that people living there can be prepared for a volcanic eruption or an earthquake.

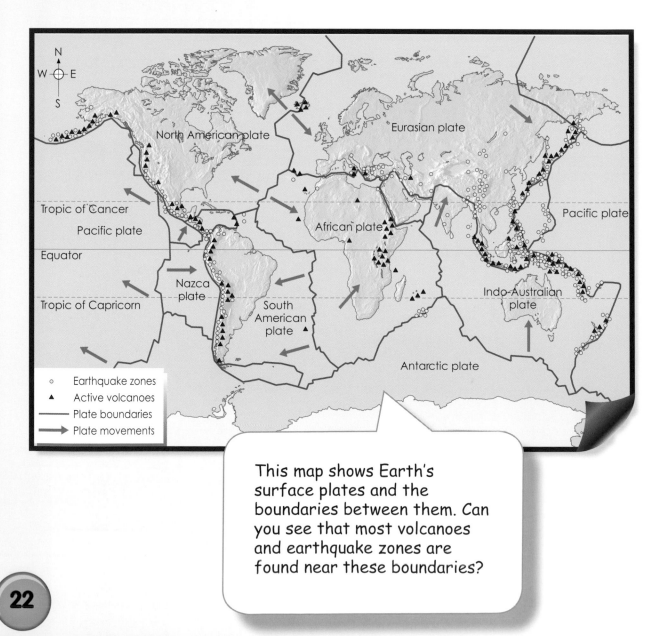

This map shows Earth's surface plates and the boundaries between them. Can you see that most volcanoes and earthquake zones are found near these boundaries?

Measuring movements

Scientists can study areas that are at risk from volcanic eruptions or earthquakes. They use maps to find the best places to measure any movement of the surface. Special instruments can be placed at these places. They detect and record any movement, and scientists can study these small movements to try to predict when a more serious movement might happen.

Many volcanoes give off huge flowing clouds of dust, ash, and rock. These flows can be mapped to make sure that no buildings are built in the way of any future flows.

Mapping Rocks and Resources

Many people need to know what types of rocks are below the ground. The study of rocks is called geology.

Rock type is very important in shaping the land. Hard rocks are slow to be worn away by wind and water. Soft rocks can be worn away quickly. Buildings and roads should only be built where the rock underneath is strong enough. Geological maps can help people to plan the best locations for building.

This is a geological map of Iceland. There are four main rock types. The white areas are large sheets of ice. Scientists have not yet mapped these rocks.

KEY

⬜	Sedimentary rock
⬛	Volcanic rock younger than 700,000 years old
⬛	Volcanic rock 700,000 to 3 million years old
⬛	Volcanic rock over 3 million years old

Finding resources

Certain rocks contain very valuable **resources** such as copper, oil, and diamonds. Geological maps can help people decide where to start looking for these resources.

This oil well is testing for oil. The engineers use geological maps to figure out where they might find oil.

NO DRILLING ALLOWED!

Many people believe that there are valuable natural resources to be found in Antarctica because of the geology of the area. However, no drilling or mining is allowed in this precious habitat.

Satellites and Maps

For hundreds of years, people made maps from the ground. They would simply look at the land and draw what they saw. They might use a high point, such as a church tower, to get a better view.

Now airplanes help us to get a **"bird's-eye view"** of the ground. This means looking down at the ground from above. Small cameras fitted to airplanes take lots of aerial photographs. Maps can be created from these aerial photographs. Satellites also help to make maps. They can take images of large areas of land.

This satellite image of Australia and southeast Asia shows vegetation in green, deserts in yellow, and mountain ranges in gray. The ocean is shades of blue, depending on how deep it is.

Geographical information systems

Satellite images can be part of a geographical information system (GIS). A GIS is a computer program. It contains lots of different types of map information for an area. These form layers of information. The GIS can work through all these layers of information, selecting the best parts for a certain purpose. It can then produce a map that contains exactly the information required.

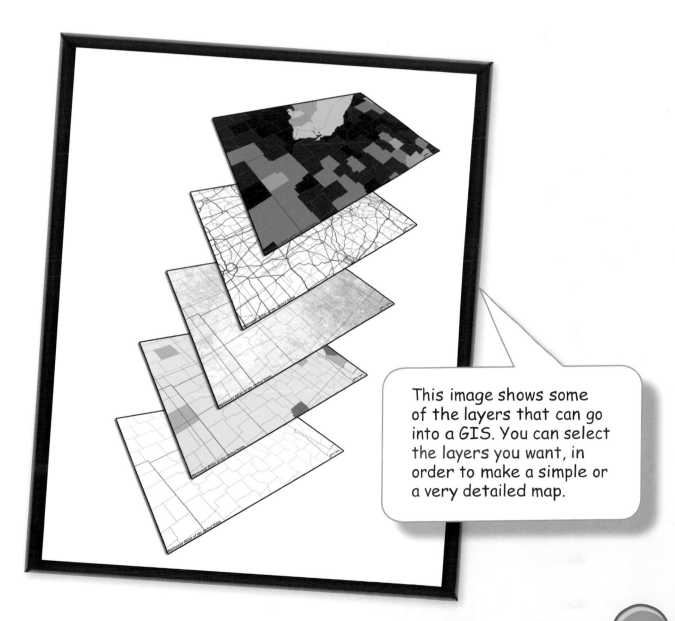

This image shows some of the layers that can go into a GIS. You can select the layers you want, in order to make a simple or a very detailed map.

Get Mapping!

Here are two maps showing land and weather. Look at the maps and the symbols and then answer the questions.

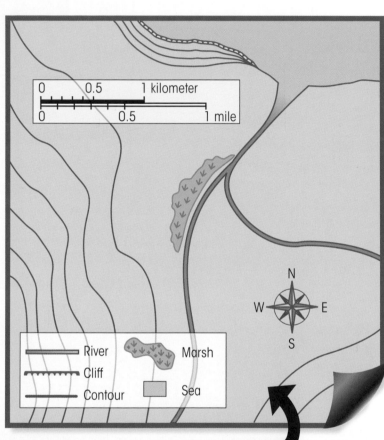

0   0.5   1 kilometer

0   0.5   1 mile

River

Cliff

Contour

Marsh

Sea

1) Look at the compass rose. This is the little symbol at the bottom-right corner of the map with four letters marked on it: N, S, E, and W. What do these letters stand for?

2) Where is the land very steep? Where is it very flat?

3) What can you see along the north edge of the coastline?

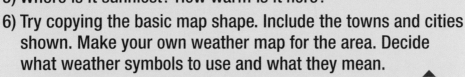

4) Describe the weather in this area. Where is it windiest? What direction is the wind blowing from?

5) Where is it sunniest? How warm is it here?

6) Try copying the basic map shape. Include the towns and cities shown. Make your own weather map for the area. Decide what weather symbols to use and what they mean.

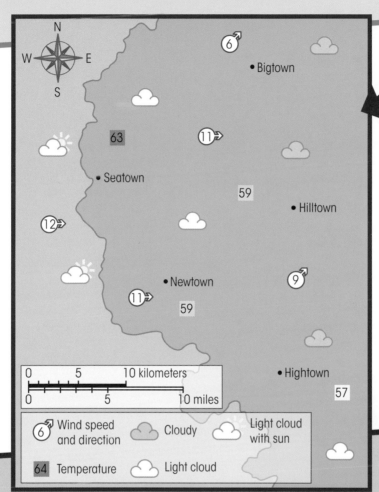

N W E S

6 Bigtown

63

11

59

Seatown

12

Hilltown

Newtown

9

11

59

Hightown

57

| 0 | 5 | 10 kilometers |
| 0 | 5 | 10 miles |

6 Wind speed and direction

Cloudy

Light cloud with sun

64 Temperature

Light cloud

Glossary

3D short for "three-dimensional"; this means having height, width, and depth. Something flat, such as a drawing, has only two dimensions.

biome area in the world with a certain climate and where certain plants and animals can live

bird's-eye view what something looks like from high above the ground

border imaginary line that separates different countries or different regions inside a country

cartographer person who makes maps

climate usual weather conditions in a place

climate zone area on Earth where the climate is the same

continent one of Earth's seven major areas of land: North America, South America, Europe, Africa, Asia, Australia, and Antarctica

contour line line on a map that follows all the land at a certain height above sea level

endangered threatened with dying out

equator imaginary circle around Earth that is halfway between the North and South Poles

isobar line on a weather map to show equal pressure

key list of symbols and an explanation of what each one represents

latitude distance between the equator and a point north or south on Earth's surface. The distance is measured in degrees.

longitude distance on Earth's surface that is east or west of the prime meridian. The distance is usually measured in degrees.

natural feature something on Earth's surface that has been created by nature—for example, a mountain

ocean current huge body of seawater that flows in the same direction and can be warm or cold

physical map map that shows the shape of the land and its natural features

political map map that shows countries and their borders and often capital cities

resource something that is of value to humans that Earth can provide

sonar short for "sound navigation and ranging"; this uses sound to find objects underwater

symbol object or picture that represents something

tectonics movement of the huge plates of rock that make up Earth's surface

thematic map map that shows information on a certain topic related to a particular area

weather forecast weather that is likely to happen in a place in the near future

Find Out More

There is a whole world of mapping waiting to be discovered! Start by looking at some other books and web sites.

Books

Henzel, Cynthia Kennedy. *Reading Maps* (On the Map). Edina, Minn.: ABDO, 2008.

Johnson, Jinny. *Maps and Mapping* (Inside Access). Boston: Kingfisher, 2007.

Oxlade, Chris. *Global Warming* (Mapping Global Issues). Mankato, Minn.: Smart Apple Media, 2012.

Snedden, Robert. *Mapping Earth from Space* (Science Missions). Chicago: Raintree, 2011.

Web sites

www.nationalatlas.gov
This U.S. government web site offers many different kinds of maps of the United States, such as maps that show different types of land, weather, and the number of people living in an area. Explore the links here to learn more about maps. You can also try to make a map yourself.

www.nationalgeographic.com/kids-world-atlas/maps.html
This National Geographic page is full of links to information about maps. The resources listed here will help you create your own maps, find maps for school reports, zoom in on different parts of the world, and much more!

weather.gov
This is the web site for the National Weather Service. You can look at maps with different kinds of forecasts throughout the country.

Index